SNAKES

A PHOTO-FACT BOOK

BY
S. TROPEA

KIDSBOOKS, INC.
7004 N. California Ave.
Chicago, Illinois 60645

Printed in the U.S.A.

Black-Tailed Rattlesnake

There are more than 4700 different kinds of snakes in the world. They come in thousands of shapes, colors and sizes. Some are fearsome and deadly, while others are timid and harmless. But only one kind has rattles—the awesome rattlesnakes.

Like all snake species, there is more than one kind of rattlesnake. The characteristic that makes them unique is shared by them all—the rattle. Rattles are located at the tip of the rattlesnake's tail. They are hollow, interlocking horny cones that produce a buzzing sound when shaken. Baby rattlers are born live with only a button at the tip of their tails. Each time the growing snake sheds its skin, a new cone is added. Since snakes moult (shed their skins) more than once a year, the number of rattles is not equal to a rattlesnake's age. Also, after a few moults, the oldest cones break off so it is rare to find a rattlesnake with more than 9 or 10 cones in its rattle.

It is not certain what purpose the rattle serves. Some herpetologists (scientists who study snakes) think it may be a lure. When it is shaken, they believe it keeps the attention of the snake's prey on the snake's tail and not on its head. Since all snakes first catch their prey with their mouths, the unsuspecting prey would not notice the snake getting ready to strike.

The black-tailed rattlesnake is venomous (poisonous). This 3- to 4-foot-long snake is not as aggressive as some other rattlers. It is usually found in the rocky, mountainous regions of the southwestern United States and in Mexico. It is normally seen at night, but may be found basking in the cooler parts of the day. Its main diet is small rodents.

Snake-Eating Snake

All snakes are meat-eaters. Depending on their size and where they live, they eat anything from insects to large mammals. There are a number of snakes that eat other snakes as a part of their diet. Some eat little else and are even immune to the highly toxic venom of pit vipers, rattlesnakes and copperheads. The red snake-eating snake in the photo is found in the rain forests of Costa Rica.

Another well-known snake-eater is the king cobra. This snake, which can grow to a length of 18 feet, produces large quantities of very potent venom that is used by scientists to make anti-snake bite serum.

Since snakes have small heads and thin bodies, small thin meals such as other snakes would seem to be a logical diet. This is not so. Relative to their size, snakes eat larger prey than any other land animal. This is due to their ability to open their mouths unusually wide and to distend (stretch wide) their bodies. Snake jaws are hinged in a way that allows them to open in the normal fashion, and also to swing down and out. At its widest, a snake can eat something that is two to three times wider than its head when its mouth is closed.

Snakes do not chew their food. They swallow their prey whole. Powerful muscles draw the victim down the snake's gullet to the stomach. To make the swallowing easier, saliva is produced to act as a lubricant. The saliva also begins the digestion process. Once in the stomach, strong digestive juices dissolve almost everything the snake eats, even bones. If a snake is frightened during the course of a meal or has to escape quickly, it will spit out its food.

Coral Snake

The coral snake family includes such very venomous snakes as cobras, kraits and mambas. They live in tropical and subtropical regions of the world and can be found in South America, Asia, Africa and Australia. There are only two species of coral snakes in North America. They are the Arizona coral snake and the eastern coral snake.

Coral snakes have brightly colored alternating bands of red and black that are separated by narrow white or yellow rings. The warning "black on yellow kill a fellow" is a reminder that the venomous coral snake has different markings than other snakes such as the scarlet snake and scarlet king snake. These two snakes mimic the coral snake and are harmless. The coral snake is not. Its bite can be fatal.

Coral snakes are often found on the surface, in tunnels or under rocks and logs. Because these snakes are mostly active at night, it is uncertain why they are so brightly colored. Some scientists believe the colors may startle a predator that uncovers a coral snake in the daytime, giving the snake time to escape.

North American coral snakes are rather small and their behavior is unpredictable. They can become very agitated when disturbed and will thrash and bite wildly. Though their fangs are short and their mouths are small, their venom is extremely potent. The 2- to 3-foot coral snake eats other snakes, lizards and frogs.

Eyelash Viper

The eyelash viper is a member of a very large family of vipers. This family contains snakes that live on the ground (terrestrial) as well as snakes that live in trees (arboreal). The eyelash viper is an example of an arboreal snake.

Arboreal snakes are often called palm vipers. They have a few simple modifications that make it easy for them to climb trees and travel from branch to branch. Some, including the mambas and vine snakes, have elongated bodies. Others, such as boas, pythons and vipers, have short prehensile (grasping) tails. They can wrap their tails around a trunk or branch to keep from falling and to assist them in climbing. Many are excellent climbers that get a "foothold" on tree bark and branches with their scales by flexing their skin muscles. Tropical arboreal snakes usually have big heads, pointed snouts and large eyes. Their coloring blends into the foliage. They are very difficult to see when they are motionless, even from a very close distance. A danger is that they can easily bite the face of anyone who walks nearby.

The eyelash viper gets its name from an area of bristly scales over its eyes. It is arboreal and is able to suspend itself in a tree by wrapping its tail around a branch. Like most vipers, it relies on camouflage to conceal it as it waits for prey to come within striking distance. It is able to snatch birds with its large open mouth while dangling. The venomous eyelash viper lives throughout Mexico and South America.

Indian Python

The Indian python is the most common and popular of the pythons. Growing to a maximum of 21 feet, it is a giant among snakes. It has been successfully bred in captivity and is considered to be quite docile.

The Indian python is a good climber and can hang from trees by its prehensile tail. Though heavy and somewhat sluggish, it will hang suspended until a meal comes along. It strikes its victims and then wraps its body around it in a series of coils. By constricting (squeezing) its prey in the coils, the snake kills by suffocation. It eats larger, warm-blooded prey, depending on its own size. Young snakes will eat mice and newly hatched chicks. Adults eat full-grown chickens and ducks and even small pigs. The largest animal ever eaten by an Indian python was a four-foot-long leopard.

Indian pythons have been known to attack people, but usually they do so only if they are provoked. They are found in Asia, from Pakistan to southern China.

The young are hatched from eggs that are kept warm by the mother in a shallow nest. She wraps herself around her 20–60 eggs and by making a twitching motion is able to raise their temperature. This is unusual because pythons, like all snakes, are cold-blooded and produce no body heat.

Newborn pythons are about two and a half feet long. They grow quickly and can reach six and one half feet in length in their first year.

Huge snakes such as pythons are vulnerable after eating large meals. When gorged with food, they can't move fast. For this reason, like all snakes, they prefer to have smaller but more frequent meals rather than large, infrequent ones.

Indian Cobra

The Indian cobra is a fast and graceful snake that is favored by snake charmers. Like other cobras, it can raise the top third of its body off the ground. It then spreads its ribs to form a hood near its head. It does this when it is annoyed and when it is going to strike. It strikes by falling forward. It can't strike farther than the length of the raised section. Even baby cobras can strike while still hatching from their eggs.

Some Indian cobras are able to spit their venom a distance of 12 feet. This is used for defense rather than attack. The fangs of spitting cobras have tiny openings in the front instead of at the ends. When venom is forced through the fangs, it sprays in the direction the head is aiming. The venom can blind its victim if it gets into the eyes.

Cobra fangs aren't retractable like viper fangs. They are shorter and remain extended all the time. A cobra bite is often deadly because its venom is more powerful, drop for drop, than viper venom. In India where the snake is common, as many as 10,000 people are bitten each year. Of these about 1,000 die. The 4- to 5-foot-long Indian cobra feeds on a diet of mice, rats, frogs, birds and eggs. They are found throughout Southeast Asia.

The Indian cobra is distinguished by markings on its hood which look like spectacles. Even though its bite is often fatal, cobras are not killed in India because they are considered holy. A myth says that the god Krishna fell asleep while visiting earth and was shaded from the hot sun by a cobra. Krishna touched the cobra with two fingers, leaving the spectacle mark as a sign of favor.

Purple Spotted Pit Viper

Pit vipers such as the purple spotted pit viper are considered by scientists to be the most highly evolved snakes. Usually short and thickset, pit vipers are recognizable by their wide, spade-shaped heads. This shape is due to large venom glands on either side of the mouth. Highly potent poison is produced in the glands. They are connected to thin, hollow fangs. When the snake bites, the venom is injected into the victim's blood. Depending on its potency, the venom stuns or kills the victim so it can be eaten.

This sophisticated system works because of another unusual adaptation. The viper's fangs are much too long to fit in its mouth and would extend outside if it wasn't for the fact that they are hinged. When the snake's jaw is closed, the fangs are retracted. They lie flat against the roof of the mouth in sheaths. When the snake strikes, it opens its jaws wide. This automatically unfolds the fangs so they are erect. When the jaw closes on a victim, the fangs penetrate whatever is bitten. After the venom is injected, the fangs are retracted.

Pit vipers are found in most parts of the world. They live in all types of habitats from mountains and deserts to forests and swamps. Most pit vipers are terrestrial (live on land), though some live in trees and have prehensile tails for grasping. Most also rely on camouflage for concealment.

The characteristic that distinguishes pit vipers from other vipers is the pair of small holes or pits on its snout. Found just behind the nostrils, the pits are heat-sensing organs that help the snake find warm-blooded animals.

Garter Snake

When you come upon a snake in North America, the chances are it will be a garter snake. They are the most widely distributed snake on the continent. They can be found from the Atlantic to the Pacific coasts in almost every region except the hot, arid deserts of the Southwest.

The name "garter snake" comes from the colorful elastic garters once used to hold up stockings. The average length of a garter snake is about 2 feet. Garter snakes prefer to live near water in marshes, meadows, woods and ditches.

Garter snakes are not poisonous. But like other snakes, they do strike and bite to defend themselves. A garter snake bite can cause swelling and sometimes severe headaches. This may be an allergic reaction. Generally they are docile, and many are kept as pets.

A peculiar but effective defense employed by many garter snakes is to release a foul-smelling substance on its attackers.

Garter snake babies are born alive from eggs kept inside the female until they are ready to hatch. As many as 85 may be born at one time. The young eat earthworms, insects, small toads and salamanders. Later they prey on small animals or birds as well as crayfish, fish and frogs.

Garter snakes can be found in northern areas and can remain active in temperatures as low as 45° F. Like many other snakes, they spend the winter hibernating together in large numbers in ground burrows and other safe places.

Ringed Tree Boa

Snakes evolved from a lizardlike ancestor millions of years ago. As lizards, they crawled over the ground on four legs. Their legs disappeared as they learned to crawl without them. Most snakes have no trace left of the legs. Boas are more primitive than most snakes. They still have two tiny bones, each one covered by a horny claw, that are located where the hind legs used to be. The claws no longer serve any purpose.

Like all snakes, the ringed tree boa has adapted crawling to suit its own needs. Some boas live in semidesert regions, but most boas live in rain forests. They spend most of their time in the treetops and come down only to hunt for food.

Boas are large and heavy snakes. Though most are only two to four feet long, others are extremely long. The largest boa, the anaconda, grows as long as 33 feet. There are over 30 different species of boas. Most are found in Africa, Asia, and Central and South America.

To move its weight, especially in trees, the boa uses its powerful prehensile tail. To climb, the boa first wraps itself around a tree trunk. Holding a firm grip with its strong tail, it then reaches up with its head to hook its neck around a branch. When the front of its body is secure, the boa loosens its tail grip and pulls itself up. It continues until it finds a suitable place to rest or to wait for prey.

Boas are nonpoisonous. When the boa strikes, it grips the animal in its mouth and quickly wraps its body around it. By constricting, the victim is squeezed until it suffocates and dies. Boas don't crush their prey, and no bones are broken. The animal is eaten whole.

Sidewinder

The sidewinder lives in the deserts of the southwestern United States and Mexico. It is a rattlesnake and is sometimes called the horned rattlesnake. The name comes from a small horn over each eye that some scientists believe may protect the eye from the sun and sand.

The sidewinder hunts at night. During the day it buries itself in the sand. Because it is rarely seen, the only evidence of its presence is the J-shaped tracks it leaves on the desert sand. The tracks are formed by the specialized locomotion it uses.

Most snakes travel over the ground in a straight line. Their bodies curve, but they move in the direction the head points. Stones, grass and rough ground give them traction to crawl. Sand is too soft. With nothing to grip, a snake would slip if it used normal snake motion.

The sidewinder and a few other snakes around the world have developed "sidewinding." With its neck on the ground, the sidewinder throws the front of its body forward in a loop. Then it twists the rest of its body off the ground and throws it forward. Before the tail portion strikes the ground, the snake places its neck on the ground and throws another loop. Only two parts of the body touch the ground as the snake moves in a forward and sideways motion. The parts that touch leave the J-mark in the sand. When the ground is firm, sidewinders move normally, like other snakes.

Sidewinders are poisonous, but their venom is considered mild. They are not a serious threat to humans, but they are deadly to the mice, kangaroo rats and lizards that are its normal diet. Like other pit vipers, the sidewinder has heat-sensitive pits in its nose that help detect warm-blooded prey.

Copperhead

Most copperheads live in the eastern part of the United States. They are pit vipers and are poisonous. The coloring of copperheads serves as camouflage and the differences reflect their habitats. Those that live in wooded areas blend into the forest floor. Those living in arid regions are able to hide easily among rocks and sand.

Like most snakes, the copperhead prefers to lie in the sun in the daytime during mild weather, and hunt at night. Its den can be found among rocky outcrops, often facing east or south for warmth.

Cold-blooded animals like snakes get their heat from their surroundings. They bask (lie in) the sun in order to raise their body temperature. When the sun gets too hot, they will seek a shady place to cool down. Their inability to produce their own heat limits their activity. In winter they are totally inactive, and even a cool evening will cause them to slow their movements.

Copperheads eat large insects, frogs, lizards and small rodents. The young wiggle their tails to attract the attention of their prey. Although copperheads are venomous, they are not aggressive. Unless they are bothered, they are not likely to strike. An angry copperhead will vibrate its tail in dry leaves or twigs to make a sound like a rattlesnake. Its bite is painful, but rarely fatal. Most snake bites in the eastern United States are by copperheads.

All photos: Animals Animals

Cover: Pacific rattler by Zig Leszczynski
Black-tailed rattler by Zig Leszczynski
Snake-eating snake by OSF/M. Fogden
Coral snake by OSF/M. Fogden
Eyelash viper by Michael Fogden
Indian python by Zig Leszczynski
Indian cobra by Zig Leszczynski
Purple spotted pit viper by Zig Leszczynski
Garter snake by Kevin Jackson
Ringed tree boa by Michael Fogden
Sidewinder by Zig Leszczynski
Copperhead by Zig Leszczynski